Existential Humanism: How to Live Authentically in Today's World

by Ronald Haines

Preface: Something is Wrong

Something is wrong with the way many people are living their lives. How do we know that? Let's consider the following facts:

The most common regret of dying people is that they didn't live their lives being true to themselves, and instead did what others expected of them.

Many people are suppressing their feelings in order to keep peace with others, and thereby settling for a mediocre existence, never becoming the person they are capable of being.

When fear of change causes people to pretend to others and to themselves that they are content, when deep within they long to laugh and have the silliness of childhood back in their lives, something is clearly wrong.

A third of Americans admitted that they regret many of the major life decisions they have made and wish they had taken more risks when making those decisions.

When asked to design their ideal life, half of Americans respond that they would like to live a life unique to their own interests instead of following a traditional path.

When people do not realize that happiness is a choice, that they can simply choose to break free of the comfort of the familiar and the established, something is definitely wrong.

Do not wait for the clarity of impending death before you realize that something is wrong in your own life. Instead, recognize that you can gain that clarity now.

Choose to live your life filled with happiness and personal satisfaction. Take control and live an authentic life with Existential Humanism.

Table of Contents

Introduction

I could have put on my scholarly hat and made this a 500 page tome, but that would have exhausted me and bored you. Today's reader looks for bite- sized nuggets written in plain English, so that is what you'll find in these pages.

Existential humanism is the tool I developed to provide a sense of what the world is all about and how the individual can fit into it without having to compromise who they are. Life is simple, but not particularly easy. I encourage you to live it, enjoy it, be a part of it, but don't diminish all the life around you by attempting to give it a reason for existing. Rather, recognize that there is no meaning to life beyond the meaning we individually give our own lives.

Chapter 1: Overview

TODAY'S ISSUE WITH RELIGION

We hear a lot in the news nowadays about the newest religion being no religion at all. Many people are abandoning their long held religious beliefs, often referring to themselves as spiritual-but-not-religious, or atheist. Established religious doctrine is simply no longer working for these people as they try to make sense of the modern world, and the resulting feeling of unrest, angst, is causing significant religious exodus.

How is it that religions that have been a source of answers and comfort for people for hundreds, in some cases thousands, of years suddenly appear to be broken? Certainly, there are multiple and varied reasons on the individual level, but by standing back and taking a big picture look the driving force behind this movement becomes quite clear. Religions arose concurrently with civilizations in more-or-less homogeneous, stable societies. But societies today are rapidly becoming less homogeneous, and people are being exposed to new information and scientific discoveries on an almost daily basis.

While increased knowledge and more information about the world is certainly a positive occurrence, in many cases it has caused people to question what their particular religions may have led them to believe, and this conflict between long held beliefs and current information encourages them to reach out for answers to calm their growing feelings of angst. I have always considered religions in a positive light in that they provide people with a sense of comfort, community and a 'track to run on' through life and give the individual a sense of who he is relative to the world at large. Unfortunately, when people today reach out to them in search of answers, the traditional solutions offered by their religious leaders frequently results in more angst, and often compounds it with a sense of guilt about "incorrect thinking" which many find they can do nothing about. Dissatisfied and not willing to simply stop thinking, these are the people who are leaving their religions in search of something that will be a better fit for them. But where can they go?

As human beings they seek answers to the big questions about life, but what religion exists for the individual who enjoys free thinking and constantly questions the nature of the world around him? According to studies, many of them are becoming atheists. But that term is most likely being misapplied in these cases since atheism isn't about the absence of religion; there are numerous secular religions in the world.

Religions provide a sense of belonging, being a part of society as a whole, to the point where people who may not believe in them often go along with them so as not to be ostracized, but doing so is also a cause of inner turmoil. Existential humanism is not about being critical of any religion; an essential part of this approach is the equal recognition of all religions and the freedom of individuals to follow whatever path they wish. A later chapter will explore what a perfect religion might look like, and provides a guide for anyone attempting to find a religion that is more suitable for them.

I present existential humanism as an alternative to religion. This approach provides satisfying answers about life, truth, infinity, and other big questions by providing for a dynamic which is missing from traditional religions.

INTRODUCING EXISTENTIAL HUMANISM

In a nutshell, existential humanism is the world view I have developed over my lifetime and it has proven to be extremely satisfying for me and those with whom I have shared it. Existential humanism provides for the inclusion of new information as it becomes available and does not cling to previous dogma, which gives it a unique dynamic. The term existential humanism is perfect because it describes what it is, a combination of various components of existentialism and humanism. But labeling anything is unfortunate because it invites preconceptions. So with that in mind I would like to first address the well-known book, *Existentialism is a Humanism*, written by Jean- Paul Sartre in 1945.

The book is actually the text of a lecture Sartre gave at The Club Maintenant in Paris in October of that year, which was his attempt to defuse negative feelings about existentialism in post-world war 2 France. The lecture itself was more correctly labeled, "Is Existentialism a Humanism?" Here is an excerpt:

"One has reproached me ridiculing a type of humanism in nausea, and now suggesting that existentialism is a form of humanism. The absurd type of humanism is to glory Man the magnificent ascribing to all men the value of the deeds of the most distinguished men. Only a dog or a horse would be in a position to declare such a judgment. But there is another humanism, the acceptance that there is only one universe, the universe of human subjectivity."

What Sartre is referring to is humanity rather than any form of humanism specifically, and he points out the inherent danger of institutionalizing humanism. We can also draw from Sartre's writings that existentialism allows for the individual to make choices, so the individual may choose to consider other humans if he wishes. But he is also free to just as easily ignore them. Existentialism, therefore, is not necessarily a humanism. However, a person who follows existential thinking and also elects to be humanistic may well be considered an existential humanist, and that is how this label has been derived.

INTRODUCING EXISTENTIALISM

Existentialism provides a philosophical component of existential humanism. It is unfortunate that existential philosophers as a whole are rather inaccessible to the general population in that they present their ideas in complex language, as if they were only talking to each other, and their ideas often come across as being about gloom and doom. If you dig into existentialism, however, you soon arrive at the realization that it is focused on individuality and freedom, and that doesn't have to be viewed in a negative light at all. In fact, Jean Paul Sartre himself had a very positive time with it in post-world war 2 Paris.

Existentialism is both exciting and liberating, and provides the vehicle for living an authentic life, the details of which are discussed in the next chapter.

INTRODUCING HUMANISM

While humanism in some form or another has been around since the ancient Greeks and currently takes on many forms, we'll take just the basic concepts from it. As a human being you are the beneficiary of all of humankind that has come before you, and in your life you have the opportunity to make a contribution to this ongoing stream of knowledge.

Unfortunately, the humanistic religions have created structures and institutions around it which take away from the individual.

Existential humanism embraces the basic concepts of humanism, specifically secular humanism, without any of these structures, and blends it with the philosophy of existentialism to create an approach to viewing the world which actually makes sense. The applicable aspects of humanism are discussed in chapter 3.

Chapter 2: Becoming Authentic

Existentialism is a philosophy of action, unlike many of the traditional philosophies which may be considered too far removed from human experience to be of any benefit to daily living. Existentialism's focus is on finding self, meaning for one's life, and accepting the personal responsibility to make choices without the help of external laws, rules, or traditions. The existentialist Jean-Paul Sartre asserted that the key defining concept of existentialism is that a person's existence occurs prior to their essence, meaning that only the individual can define who he or she really is. Since existentialism is about defining oneself, it is an optimistic and liberating philosophy.

AUTHENTICITY

At the heart of existentialism is the search for authenticity, which is the degree to which one is true to one's own self in spite of external pressures. An authentic action is a choice which comes about as the result of personal understanding and is taken consistent with one's true self, rather than merely acting from conformity according to the society in which the person lives. Yet we are born within our respective societies and raised to accept the associated conventions, relationships, and in many cases the religions that characterize them. As the philosopher Martin Heidegger so aptly stated, "We are thrown into pre-made worlds."

Our parents and teachers infuse us with what we need to know in order to get by in the societies that we live in, and often pressure us into behaving according to this established norm. But if we just blindly follow those rules and expectations, which in many cases means we would be acting inauthentically, then we may begin to suffer psychologically as a result. It becomes important, therefore, to define who we really are in order to be able to live an authentic life. And in order to achieve authenticity, one must face reality and form their own opinions of existence.

FREEDOM AND RESPONSIBILITY

The first principle of existentialism is that humans have no purpose other than what they create for themselves, and a major theme of existentialism is that every human is a free individual. Jean-Paul Sartre explained it this way:

"What does this mean? If one considers a manufactured object, say a book or a paper- knife, one sees that it has been made to serve a definite purpose. It has an essence, the sum of its purpose and qualities, which precedes its existence. The concept of man in the mind of God is comparable to the concept of paper-knife in the mind of the artisan. My atheist existentialism is rather more coherent. It declares that God does not exist, yet there is still a being in whom existence precedes essence, a being which exists before being defined by any concept, and this being is man or, as Heidegger puts it, human reality. That means that man first exists, encounters himself, and emerges in the world, to be defined afterwards."

Since we arrive in the world having no predetermined purpose, we are the ones to determine what our lives will be all about. Humans not only have the individual freedom to determine what their own lives will be, but they must also take the responsibility to do so. Sartre summed it up by stating,

"Man is condemned to be free; because once thrown into the world, he is responsible for everything he does."

EXISTENTIAL HUMANISM: HOW TO LIVE AUTHENTICALLY IN TODAY'S WORLD

Freedom, then, is fundamental to being human, and Erich Fromm eloquently stated that freedom is something that we must either embrace or escape from. He observed that embracing our freedom was healthy, whereas escaping from freedom was the root of psychological conflicts.

The societies that we live in, however, tend to encourage escaping from freedom by promising a feeling of comfort in return, and as a result many people do so. A common escape from freedom can be obtained through conformity. By changing oneself to fit the perception of society's preferred type of personality, one can displace the burden of choice from oneself to society. To do this a person might tie their identity to an image which corresponds to some sort of social norm, such as becoming a plumber or a banker for example. The person then acts according to the image they have of how a plumber or bank manager should act.

Another means of escape is through authoritarianism. This means relinquishing control of oneself to another person. Or, in the case of some theic religions, to a deity or supernatural being.

By submitting one's freedom to someone or something else, individual freedom of choice can be removed almost entirely.

Human beings are free, but the responsibility resting on the individual to create oneself and then be willing to act accordingly can be daunting, and these comfort mechanisms that society offers does appeal to the majority. But these people who do escape from freedom are denying their true selves in the process. They may live exemplary lives, but studies have shown that over a third of them will lie on their deathbeds regretting that they had not followed their dreams or taken more risks with their lives.

Now this does not mean that all acting in accordance with social norms is inauthentic. The point is about the attitude one takes to one's own freedom and responsibility, and the extent to which one acts in accordance with their freedom. It is perfectly reasonable that one can act within the norms of society and still be a free, self-determined individual.

THE MEANING OF LIFE

If one recognizes that humans are inherently free, accepts the responsibility to define their own life, and attempts to live authentically, then he or she will easily come to terms with the fact that there is no meaning to life beyond the meaning we individually give our own lives. This meaninglessness also encompasses the amorality or unfairness of the world at large, which Albert Camus called the absurdity of life. There is no such thing as a good person or a bad person, and what happens in life simply happens. So, because of the world's absurdity where anything can happen to anyone, an unforeseen event could plummet anybody into direct confrontation with the absurd at any point in time.

For many people, life's absurdity and the realization that life is meaningless until we give it meaning may prompt them to choose to live an inauthentic life, inauthenticity being the denial to live in accordance with one's freedom, by embracing social norms and convincing themselves to believe that some form of determinism is true. This will be addressed further in the chapter on belief and faith.

ANGST AND FEAR

Angst is a term commonly associated with existentialism and is generally considered to be a negative feeling arising from the awareness of human freedom, responsibility and the inherent lack of meaning in life. The archetypal example given is the experience a person has while standing on the edge of a cliff where one not only fears falling off, but also dreads the possibility of throwing themselves off. In this nothing is holding me back scenario a person senses the lack of predetermination to either throw oneself off or to stand still, and thus one experiences true freedom.

Existentialists often stress the importance of angst as signifying the inherent insecurity about the consequences of one's actions, and to the fact that, in experiencing freedom as angst, one also realizes that one is fully responsible for the consequences of their actions. There is nothing or nobody that they can blame if something goes wrong. A positive, and pervasive, theme in the works of existentialist philosophy, however, is to persist through the angst and accept freedom as an exhilarating positive; something that opens endless possibilities.

Sometimes the awareness of freedom and its associated responsibility can bring about a case of fear which may cause people to turn away from their course of action by using excuses that external forces are somehow standing in the way of what they otherwise would be doing. It is important to recognize that these 'reasons' are simply delusions.

Fear is different to angst because fear has an object, so in the case of fear one can take definitive measures to remove the object of fear and thereby eliminate that feeling. The simplest way to cure fear is to take action, and by starting with small steps and developing a bias towards action and accomplishment, fear can effectively be overcome. Through action one also obtains control of a situation, and it is that sense of control that finally erases fear.

Understanding that fears are self-made delusions, the question really becomes whether an individual is willing to allow these delusions to prevent them from living the life they want to live. Do they want to end up facing the end of their lives regretting what they did not do, or would they prefer to approach the end of their lives with a sense of satisfaction that they had accomplished what they set out to do?

CREATIVITY

Because authenticity is about an individual's relationship with the world, it is necessarily subjective and cannot be arrived at by simply repeating a set of actions or taking up a set of positions. In this manner, authenticity is connected with creativity: the impetus to action arises from within the person in question and is not externally imposed. Soren Kierkegaard's summary explains it nicely:

"The subjective thinker's form, the form of his communication, is his style...His form must first and last be related to existence, and in this regard he must have at his disposal the poetic, the ethical, the dialectical, the religious. Subordinate character, setting, etc., which belong to the well balanced character of the esthetic production, are in themselves breadth; the subjective thinker has only one setting—existence—and has nothing to do with localities and such things. The setting is not the fairyland of the imagination, where poetry produces consummation, nor is the setting laid in England, and historical accuracy is not a concern. The setting is inwardness in existing as a human being"

Creativity is the product of an individual's outward expression, a person's communication with the world, but as Sartre so eloquently put it:

"It is man who conceives himself, who propels himself towards existence. Man becomes nothing other than what is actually done, not what he will want to be."

The only thing that matters is results, what you actually do. So if it your image of yourself is an artist or a writer or a musician you must create in order to communicate that to the world.

Looking at this another way, one realizes that genius is only known by the product. Michelangelo said that he saw the statue of David inside a block of stone, but it was only after he chipped away the 'non-David' parts that people saw his genius. Similarly you may have a masterpiece inside you, but unless it sees the light of day you will remain an unknown. The world does not care how smart or educated you might be, and in the end none of that matters. The words of the vocal group Steely Dan encapsulate this well:

"You been tellin' me you're a genius since you were seventeen. In all the time I've known you I still don't know what you mean"

RATIONALITY

Existentialists oppose definitions of human beings as primarily rational, and assert that people make decisions based on subjective meaning rather than pure rationality. The rejection of reason as the source of meaning is a common theme of existentialist thought. Rationality and reason are tools which are properly utilized when dealing with the natural world and applied to science and truth, but they do not apply to self because a person's essence is purely subjective.

DESPAIR AND HOPE

If a person escapes from their freedom using one of the mechanisms mentioned previously they are putting themselves at risk of falling into despair.

Despair is the loss of hope in reaction to a breakdown in one or more of the defining qualities of one's self or identity, and is often referred to as an existential crisis because it produces angst. So, should the absurdity of life take away the external mechanism a person has latched onto, or they find they can no longer believe in their chosen deity, a person may find themselves plunged into despair.

It is in relation to the concept of this devastating awareness of meaninglessness that Albert Camus, in his work, The Myth of Sisyphus, claimed that there is only one truly serious philosophical problem, and that is suicide.

Similarly, Fromm coined the term 'destructiveness' to describe a process in which a person attempts to eliminate others or the world as a whole, all to escape from freedom rather than face it. Fromm wrote:

"The destruction of the world is the last, almost desperate attempt to save myself from being crushed by it."

Suicide is, of course, a drastic means to deal with the trauma of being suddenly propelled into a state of angst. Rather, the existential solution to despair would, basically, be to re- group. In the Myth of Sisyphus, for example, Camus insists that one must persevere in spite of the absurdity, and, "Imagine Sisyphus happy."

We do this by looking inside ourselves. Our subjectivity allows us to realize the possibility that we really can have the life we want, and that is the definition of hope. By choosing hope one decides to take back control of their life, but in order to choose this hope one then must also accept their freedom.

Existentialism, then, helps people avoid living their lives in ways that put them in the perpetual danger of having everything meaningful break down.

ALONENESS AND COMMUNITY

Existentialism places us alone, and as unique individuals we accept that. But in the recognition that there are thousands of other people in the same situation we next introduce the human part of existential humanism. Modern communication technology permits us to join in the community of other 'alone people' to learn and share from each other. This concept of this unique community is further discussed in the chapter on humanism.

ACHIEVING AUTHENTICITY

A person who strives to live an authentic life must also recognize that there is not going to be an end product, no point at which one might say they have arrived. Personal authenticity involves subjective ideals which are necessarily revaluated on a continuous basis as new information becomes available. Our identity is always going to be multidimensional and dynamic, so our authenticity is always going to be a work in progress. Authenticity, then, may be best accomplished by setting life goals and focusing on the process rather than the end result, recognizing that the freedom and pleasure of existential living is not in the achievement of the goal but in the path to getting there. And when you do achieve one goal there will always be another. Frederick Nietzsche actually nailed this concept nicely when he wrote:

"Man is a rope stretched between the animal and the Superman — a rope over an abyss. A dangerous crossing, a dangerous wayfaring, a dangerous looking-back, a dangerous trembling and halting. What is great in man is that he is a bridge and not a goal." Where you fully experience that sense of control and freedom is when you are actually on your journey; that place where there is no room to dwell on angst and despair while you are spanning the abyss between what you left behind and the splendors that lie ahead of you. That is life."

Chapter 3: Embrace Your Humanity

Erich Fromm wrote that the person who accepts their freedom, whom he called the individualized person, may often feel left without the primary ties of belonging, and warns that as a result:

"Powerful tendencies arise to escape from freedom into submission or some kind of relationship to man and the world which promises relief, even if it deprives the individual of his freedom."

In order to remain authentic, then, it is important to have a solution which Fromm called unity, a sense of oneness between the individual and the natural and human world outside. He went on to say:

"There is only one possible, productive solution for the relationship of individualized man with the world: his active solidarity with all men and his spontaneous activity, love and work, which unite him again with the world, not by primary ties but as a free and independent individual."

In this chapter we examine humanism as a means to provide the individualized person with the abovementioned unity, the ability for an individual to be an active participant in the world without losing their freedom.

WHAT IS HUMANISM?

Humanism embraces the ability of the individual to bring advances to society using reason in the pursuit of knowledge, and as such may well be referred to as 'a religion based on reason.'

Rather than identify the many different types of humanism which range from the traditional religious, including Christian, to the agnostic and atheist, or even make a distinction between what is called religious humanism and secular humanism (which could still be called a religion), we will simply consider here the core principles of what humanism is actually all about in just three parts.

First, humanism deals with the natural world and recognizes that humans are part and product of nature itself, with a heritage that goes back to when life first appeared on our planet 3.8 billion years ago. Erich Fromm introduced the term biophilia, or love of life, to describe this human orientation of being attracted to all that is alive and vital.

Second, humanists use reason and question everything, both religious and secular, in their search for truth and challenge accepted doctrines rather than simply accepting established creed. This concept was well stated by Salman Rushdie in his Satanic Verses:

"...there is an old, old conflict between the secular view of the world and the religious view of the world, and particularly between texts which claim to be divinely inspired and texts which are imaginatively inspired. . . . I distrust people who claim to know the whole truth and who seek to orchestrate the world in line with that one true truth. I think that's a very dangerous position in the world. It needs to be challenged..."

Consider how much of human progress has been in defiance of religion or of the accepted natural order. This emphasis on rationality in no way puts humanists in conflict with existential thought, however. On the contrary, intuition, hunches, speculation, and flashes of inspiration, products of the creative mind so prized by existentialists, while not considered to be valid means to acquire knowledge, are embraced by humanists because they are the sources of ideas that will often lead to new ways of looking at the world. These ideas, when assessed rationally using the scientific method, often lead to alternative approaches for solving problems.

Third, humanism provides a sense of belonging to the world by emphasizing that we are the beneficiaries of the collective knowledge of all of the humans that came before us, and that if we wish to we have the ability to contribute to this ever lengthening legacy of humankind. Relishing the adventure of being part of new discoveries, seeking new knowledge, exploring new options, and then sharing what we have learned with others forms the commonality that connects humanists together. The products of our creativity and rational thinking are what enable us to establish ties with the world at large.

HISTORY OF HUMANISM

A lot of what one hears about humanism makes it sound like a modern concept, and due to the institutionalized structure and activities of so many humanist groups and religions it may even appear that humanism could have been something developed as an alternative to Christianity and other religions. In reality, the origins of humanism actually predate Christianity and can be found in Ancient Greece, and we might consider Socrates as one of the first advocates of humanism. Rather can claiming to know what truth was, for example, Socrates claimed to know nothing and instead created a method for questioning everything. He questioned the rules, he created the cross-examination method of inquiry, and he died advocating human rights and the rule of law. Rather than saying he knew what the truth was, Socrates provided us with a method for searching and finding it on our own. This questioning methodology is really a key principle behind humanism.

So, what happened? By the second and third centuries, Christianity had developed into a strong religious and political force and was focused on stamping out paganism and what they considered to be heresy. The Christian evangelists each reiterated in their gospels that, "If you are not with us, you are against us," which set the stage for replacing much of the Greek influences by creating an 'us-versus-them' mentality amongst their followers.

One of the most prominent Christian activists at that time was Tertullian (155-255 CE), a lawyer in Roman Africa who converted to Christianity around 198 CE. He actively spoke out against the Greek philosophers and referred to them as the "patriarchal forefathers of the heretics." He is remembered today for his famous statement, "What has Athens to do with Jerusalem," by which he promoted the position that Christians were not offending anyone by speaking out against pagan Greek thought and philosophy because he said that the bible was the source of truth.

It is interesting to note, then, that Tertullian's most remembered contribution to Christianity was the Trinity, which was actually a re-wording of Plato's tripartite theory of the soul. Since Tertullian so adamantly professed to have disconnected himself from Greek thinking and philosophy, he probably did this without realizing it. It does provide a wonderful example of underscoring a humanist point that we build and make connections with what we have learned in our past.

Effectively stifled during the Dark Ages, humanism appeared next in the Middle Ages with Medieval Islam, which then paved the way for Renaissance humanism, which at that time had become an intellectual movement in Europe.

It was during the Renaissance when the split between reason and Christianity took place, resulting in the appearance of the early stages of the more modern Secular Humanism. The subsequent phrase describing humanism, including secular humanism, as the religion of humanity is sometimes attributed to the American founding father, Thomas Paine.

EXISTENTIAL HUMANISM: HOW TO LIVE AUTHENTICALLY IN TODAY'S WORLD

One of the first of now so many structured humanist organizations was The British Humanistic Religious Association, which was formed in 1853 in London.

EXISTENTIAL HUMANISM VERSUS HUMANISM

Since they all subscribe to the basic tenets of humanism, why not simply go along one of the many humanistic religions that exist in the world today? At issue is that they are institutionalized, hierarchal organizations more focused on the group than the individual participant.

If you go on line to the American Humanist Association, for example, you'll see the Humanist Manifesto and the things that they are doing, such as lobbying, to promote 'humanist' causes, and they're asking for your money to help them promote themselves. Existential humanism is interested in contributing to humanity from the perspective of benefiting the individual, not contributing to humanist organizations who are basically acting in the same way as any other organized religion. While having nothing against them or any other religion, and recognizing they are no doubt meeting the needs of many people, existential humanism takes the position that one cannot institutionalize anything without perverting it and is instead interested in a more uncorrupted form of humanism.

Chapter 4: Religion

Why does a person subscribe to a particular religion? For some it is because they absolutely believe in it while for others it is that they were brought up to follow a particular doctrine when they were a child and continue to do so as a matter of rote. This decision may be further reinforced by social and societal associations. Those that follow a religion because of something other than an ardent belief in it, however, undoubtedly find themselves questioning it from time to time. They may harbor unspoken doubts as to the existence of God or gods and the afterlife with its designations of heaven and hell. They may even wonder if the people who are written about in the religious texts actually existed, and if they did, did they really live the lives that are ascribed to them.

The problem these questioners encounter is when they ask about their 'crises of faith' they are so often told they should obey and not question, to simply 'believe' and that 'the ways of their particular god are so mysterious' that they cannot know the reasons. Christianity, a religion that provides us with many such supernatural points that go against logic, for example, is quick to condemn the questioners within their ranks. Perhaps the most persuasive reason they use to keep people in the fold is something along the lines of, "what if it is true, do you want to take the risk of a fiery hell?" That, combined with the loss of Christmas, undoubtedly keeps untold thousands within the Christian ranks. But how many of these people still question in secret? How many have their doubts and are feeling unfulfilled?

There are a growing number of people leaving theist religions and declaring themselves to be atheists. Science provides researched explanations and many rational reasons for not subscribing to a theist religion, but while hard facts and logic are extremely compelling there are two obstacles causing many of the doubters to remain clinging to their old beliefs.

Perhaps the biggest reason is the negative connotation that many societies associate with being an atheist, making those people who might wish to identify as atheist concerned about being ostracized by friends and family if they are no longer part of the group.

A second reason is because declaring oneself an atheist and dropping out of the theist mainstream does not leave anything to address the angst that is so often associated with the resultant void. Some of these new atheists find that joining one of the many groups promoting atheism, which are very similar to the humanist religions mentioned in the last chapter, may resolve this for them.

Many of the individuals who find their religion no longer works for them are in search of a different religion that will, and they will tend to hang on to what they have until they can find a replacement rather than going it alone in having no religion at all.

In this chapter we will first define what religion actually is, then take a look at why religions fail, and finally will identify what the components of an ideal religion would be.

DEFINING RELIGION

What is religion? The common answer would depend upon who you asked. If you asked that question in Europe or the Americas you might get a definition of Christianity, whereas in China the answer might be Buddhism or in the Middle East it would be Islam. So, what is first needed is a broad definition that they would all fit into, or a working definition of what religion actually is.

EXISTENTIAL HUMANISM: HOW TO LIVE AUTHENTICALLY IN TODAY'S WORLD

1. Religion has no requirement for God or gods

If you ask people on the street how they would define religion a common response, especially where Abrahamic religions are popular, might be that religion requires a belief in God. However, there are many atheistic religions in the world, such as Buddhism, and in the United States of America the government recognizes atheism itself as a religion. Since atheism is discussed in the next chapter, we will just gloss over it here, and for the purposes of a universal definition we will conclude that God, gods or other supernatural entities are not necessary components of a religion.

2. Religion has no requirement for belief or faith

Another response a person may give is that religion consists of a belief system. However, humanist religions and others who extol questioning actually shun the concept of belief. Belief and faith are certainly part of many religions, and they are discussed more fully in the belief and faith chapter, but for the purposes of a universal definition we can conclude that belief is not a requirement.

3. Religion provides answers

Perhaps a more fundamental approach is not to analyze what religion is, but to examine why it exists. What is the benefit to having religion in the first place?

It may well be argued that humans have an innate need to ask questions about everything, an almost insatiable drive to search for answers about how the individual fits in to the world at large. Throughout history religions have arisen in an attempt to provide the answer to this and the other big questions about life in general. They developed from within various cultures and reflect the body of knowledge available to those people at that time. Religion, then, provides the individual with answers in the form of a structured view of the world.

4. Religion provides community

Humans are social creatures, and religion is a social construct offering the individual a sense of belonging, or community, with other people with like minds by providing them with a shared world view. Religion, then, can be broadly defined as a shared world view which provides the individual with answers to life's questions and a sense of community.

WHY RELIGIONS FAIL

As religions develop over time, they become hierarchical institutions and soon become focused on the institution itself rather than the individuals they were originally intended to serve. They also elevate certain members of their societies into privileged 'priest classes' who then develop self-serving resistance to change and promote an authoritative position of the religion over the followers. By providing only static solutions they fail to allow for the dynamic of change as new information is discovered. Rather than seeking fresh answers to new questions, these religions instead fall back on established dogma and view alternative ideas or emerging religions as threats which they feel compelled to oppose. Often by force or exclusion from the society itself.

Another reason that people become dissatisfied with their religion is that as religious institutions become more intolerant, they cause their followers to fall into an 'us versus them' mentality and often try to deprive them of the freedom to associate with those who have conflicting views without condemnation. Simone de Beauvoir, in her book, *The Ethics of Ambiguity*, argues that embracing our own personal freedom requires us to fight for the freedoms of all. This sentiment can appropriately be used when discussing freedom of religion and strongly suggests that to be successful, a religion should also recognize other religions and respect the choices made by individuals to subscribe to them.

THE IDEAL RELIGION

As mentioned above, humans have the need to ask questions about everything, an insatiable desire to search for truth. But most religions provide only static answers and cling to established dogmas that do not allow for the dynamic of change as new information is discovered. An ideal religion would be flexible enough to embrace and incorporate these changes, or help guide the individual to their own answers by providing them with the means to seek knowledge and truth on their own.

Religions are able to accomplish this by employing the methods of questioning inherent in the scientific method, and in fact many religions have done so in the past until the resulting answers caused people to question the core principles of what their particular religion was about. A good example can be seen with Christianity during the first millennium where 'science' was conducted by the church and continued until the time of the Renaissance and people such as Galileo began to create a rift.

Using the working definition of religion and understanding why a religion can fail as described above, we can then define the ideal religion as one which will have the following five characteristics:

1. Satisfies an individual's need for knowledge about their relationship with the world.

2. Is focused on the individual's needs rather than on preserving the group.

3. Provides a shared worldview with others.

4. Is flexible and allows for updates as new information becomes available.

5. Is tolerant of other points of view and treats all humans with respect.

This serves as an easy checklist for either evaluating any prospective religion or a guideline for creating a new one, if one were so inclined.

Alternatively, existential humanism may work for you as an alternative to religion. This approach provides satisfying answers about life, truth, infinity, and other big questions and provides room for change as new information is discovered, a dynamic which is missing from established religions.

Chapter 5: Atheist Perspective

Certainly, existential humanism is atheism by most definitions, but what does that actually mean? Today's definition of an atheist is usually considered to be someone who doesn't believe in God, a lack of belief in gods, or a belief that there is no God, all of which betray the theistic influence of society at large. Some atheists accept these definitions which, especially in a Christian environment, can present them as taking an anti-God position and adds antagonistic to the already derogatory connotation for them.

But it isn't the use of the word 'God' or 'gods' that atheists should be resisting. Most atheists probably don't really care either way about other people's gods. It is the use of the word 'belief' that is not appropriate in this context. Belief implies accepting something without proof or going along with the dictates of an authority, where an atheist has no such belief system. This concept of belief, and also faith, will be explored further in a later chapter. In this chapter we will examine what an atheist actually is and how that term came about, take a look at atheism as a religion, consider three broad categories of atheists, and discuss how an existential humanist might respond when asked whether they believe in God.

WHAT IS AN ATHEIST

The trouble with the term 'atheist' is that it is a word derived from a theist perspective and is really a word that should not exist because it is merely a reflection of a cultural bias. Culturally, what the majority of people in a society accept is considered to be the norm, and so anything outside that norm is then given a label. For an example of this, let us consider watermelons. Did you ever see a sign in an American grocery store for a seeded watermelon? That term comes about as the result of the perception of what is considered to be normal by a society's standards. Years ago, when you went to a grocery store all of the watermelons on display had seeds in them, but then seedless watermelons were developed. The seedless varieties became so popular that when you go to a supermarket today the chances are that any watermelons that are available for purchase will be seedless. If a grocer has some natural watermelons to put out for purchase, they are then labeled as 'seeded watermelons' so as not to upset the consumer who is expecting one without seeds. The implication here is that these are somehow aberrant melons since seedless is what is primarily expected of a watermelon. In its natural state a watermelon has seeds, but in American culture a watermelon with seeds has become something of an anomaly.

In the same vein, let's turn our attention to humans. A baby has no concept of god or gods when born, and only learns of them through indoctrination. If left to grow up naturally without this culturally biased input, the adult he or she becomes would subsequently be labeled by society as an atheist. Yet, in reality they are just a naturally occurring human being. So, in the same way that the term seeded watermelon is rather silly and should not exist, the term atheist should not exist either. A natural watermelon has seeds, so a variety that has been manipulated to not have them should be correctly labeled as a seedless watermelon and the naturally occurring one simply referred to as a watermelon, or a natural watermelon. A person who believes in god, gods, or other supernatural entities, then, should be rightfully called a theist human or a theist person, as opposed to a naturally occurring human. We could eliminate a lot of confusion in society if we simply abolished the word atheist and replaced it with the term natural human or natural person. The atheist label, then, is really quite meaningless. The only similarity between one atheist and another would be the same as comparing one human being to another. Outside of cultural bias, an atheist is simply a naturally occurring human.

ATHEISM

The term atheist we described above refers to an individual and carries with it no implication that he or she subscribes to atheism. For the purpose of definition, the term atheism here is used to describe a non-theistic organization, which we classify as a religion (as does the government of the United States of America) in that they provide their membership with a sense of community and the means to find answers to life's questions. If you do an internet search for atheism you will find that the organizations listed in the results look very similar to many of the humanist groups, especially the secular humanist organizations, mentioned earlier. These atheism groups, like many other religious organizations, are asking for donations and requesting that you join them in order to help promote their group.

While these assorted atheism organizations can be categorized amongst the other non-theistic religions in the world, they do deserve to be differentiated in that they are generally active, outreaching religions, as opposed to many of the other non-theistic religions, such as Buddhism, which tend to be more passive.

HISTORY OF THE ATHEIST LABEL

Te term atheist initially appeared in ancient Greek writing as "one who denies the gods." There doesn't appear to have been a discussion back then of whether the Greek gods were real or not. Rather, some people simply got along without them, taking what we might refer to today as more of an agnostic position in that the gods had no meaning to their lives. However, as Greek society progressed, being considered an atheist started to carry a negative connotation and grew to where it began to also have legal connotations. One of the charges brought against Socrates, for instance, accused him of being an atheist.

In ancient Rome the term atheist further developed to mean "against the gods" and being an atheist was therefore considered disruptive to a society in which gods played such a large and vital role. Curiously (by modern standards), the biggest atheist threat to Rome was the Christian cult because they were attempting to replace the Roman gods with their own God, which was an attack on the very fabric of Roman society. It was from here that the current, negative connotation of atheists being a force against society came from.

TYPES OF ATHEISTS

While atheists certainly do not fall into any sort of homogeneous category, if we consider them from the perspective of their attitude towards the supernatural they can be broken down into three very broad categories.

Militant Atheists

The militant atheists are probably the only sub-category that would actually embrace the 'atheist' term and be likely to subscribe to an atheism religion. This is a group that tends to be actively anti-god and frequently present themselves as the sparring partners of the evangelical, militant theists in political battles.

Agnostics

EXISTENTIAL HUMANISM: HOW TO LIVE AUTHENTICALLY IN TODAY'S WORLD

The largest atheist sub-category are most likely the agnostics. Perhaps the best example of what an agnostic is was presented by Bertrand Russell using his teapot analogy. Here is an excerpt:

"Many orthodox people speak as though it were the business of sceptics to disprove received dogmas rather than of dogmatists to prove them. This is, of course, a mistake. If I were to suggest that between the Earth and Mars there is a china teapot revolving about the sun in an elliptical orbit, nobody would be able to disprove my assertion provided I were careful to add that the teapot is too small to be revealed even by our most powerful telescopes. But if I were to go on to say that, since my assertion cannot be disproved, it is intolerable presumption on the part of human reason to doubt it, I should rightly be thought to be talking nonsense. If, however, the existence of such a teapot were affirmed in ancient books, taught as the sacred truth every Sunday, and instilled into the minds of children at school, hesitation to believe in its existence would become a mark of eccentricity and entitle the doubter to the attentions of the psychiatrist in an enlightened age or of the Inquisitor in an earlier time."

The key thing about taking an agnostic approach is the recognition that the burden of proof of a thing falls to the person making the claim. It is not up to the listener to disprove it, but the agnostic may at least be willing to listen to the argument.

Absolute Atheists

The third sub-category is made up of the absolute atheists who simply neither care about the gods of other people nor are critical of those who believe in the supernatural; it simply isn't even up for discussion. While considered an agnostic, Bertrand Russell would probably put himself in this category based on this passage that he wrote:

"I ought to call myself an agnostic; but, for all practical purposes, I am an atheist. I do not think the existence of the Christian God any more probable than the existence of the Gods of Olympus or Valhalla. To take another illustration: nobody can prove that there is not between the Earth and Mars a china teapot revolving in an elliptical orbit, but nobody thinks this sufficiently likely to be taken into account in practice. I think the Christian God just as unlikely."

Most of the agnostics and the absolute atheists would likely nowadays prefer a different label than atheist be applied to them because of the derogatory implication of the term. Since natural human has not (yet) replaced it, perhaps the term existential humanist may provide these people with a better description of their perspective.

THE ATHEIST EXISTENTIAL HUMANIST

How does an existential humanist interact with the world? If you are an existential humanist what would your response be if someone, perhaps accusingly, asks if you are an atheist? The best, non- antagonistic response would of course be, "I am an existential humanist," and depending on who you are taking to this will then elicit one of two responses.

If you are dealing with a militant theist, they might counter with, "Do you believe in God or not?" In any situation where someone asks if you believe in god it is important not to direct your answer to the god part, otherwise you will be set up for either conflict or attempted coercion. The best way to answer is with some version of, "As far as belief goes, I much prefer to question and learn, rather than just blindly accepting something. In that way I can uncover my own truths."

You could leave it at that, or if you wished you could also then add, "Now, as far as the other part of your question I consider the idea of God to be something rather fanciful, a childhood story like the Easter Bunny and Father Christmas, and I put all such ideas in that same category. But I don't have anything against those who do believe in God, or gods, or any other supernatural entities for that matter."

The second type of response to when you say you are an existential humanist might come from someone who follows up by asking, "What's that?" This moves into a discussion where you can explain that you are free to define your own life without the burdens of superstition impacting on your life. You can tell this person that you question things, learning as you go, which makes you a perpetual student of life, and hopefully will enable you to make a contribution to the ongoing progression of humanity. This approach may even result in a pleasant conversation with that person, rather than what might have otherwise been an antagonistic encounter.

Recognizing yourself as a natural person can result in a tremendous feeling of liberation, as experienced by the American agnostic, Robert G. Ingersoll, who stated:

"...When I became convinced that the universe is natural, that all the ghosts and gods are myths, there entered into my brain, into my soul, into every drop of my blood the sense, the feeling, the joy of freedom. The walls of my prison crumbled and fell. The dungeon was flooded with light and all the bolts and bars and manacles became dust. I was no longer a servant, a serf, or a slave. There was for me no master in all the wide world, not even in infinite space. I was free-free to think, to express my thoughts-free to live my own ideal, free to live for myself and those I loved, free to use all my faculties, all my senses, free to spread imagination's wings, free to investigate, to guess and dream and hope, free to judge and determine for myself . . . I was free! I stood erect and fearlessly, joyously faced all worlds...."

Chapter 6: Belief and Faith

WHAT IS BELIEF?

The simplest definition of belief is a state of mind where a person accepts something to be the case without there being any evidence to support that position, and even to automatically dismiss conflicting evidence when presented with it. Most religions have identifiable, and in some cases exclusive, sets of beliefs.

Many people take comfort in bestowing meaning on unexplained natural events rather than accept the absurdity of the world. In an often chaotic world, religious beliefs can provide them with that meaning and comfort, resulting in people having the tendency to cling tightly to their religious beliefs.

Religious beliefs often relate to the existence and worship of a deity or deities who provide some sort of intervention in the universe and human life, or are based on the teachings of a spiritual leader.

It is important to recognize that belief has nothing to do with truth, which is discussed in another chapter. Truth requires open minded questioning, which is antithetical to belief, whereas the purpose of religious belief is to guide action. Here is a brief synopsis of types of belief systems:

Fundamental Belief Systems

Religious fundamentalism is a belief that follows strict adherence to the interpretation of religious writings. Believers here generally maintain traditional understanding of the texts and are distrustful of any new revelations or alternate interpretations.

Orthodox Belief Systems

Religious orthodoxy is a belief that closely follows the edicts of a prevailing religious authority. Examples of this type of belief system are the Eastern Orthodox Church of Christianity and the Catholic Church, both of which consider themselves as the true heir to the Early Christian beliefs and practices, as well as Orthodox Judaism.

Modern Belief Systems

The Renaissance, and later the Enlightenment, led to people challenging religious authority and the prevailing beliefs associated with the established churches. The response to this was the creation of Reform Judaism and various denominations of Christianity which interpret the religious writings rather than simply accepting them.

Blended Belief Systems

Some religions blend the views of a variety of different religions or traditional beliefs into a unique fusion which suits their particular experience and context. Unitarian Universalism is an example of a blended religion, combining elements of Jewish, Christian and Humanist religions.

Other Belief Systems

In spite of their being strongly condemned by the early Christian Churches, many early religions such as occultism, animism, paganism, and other folk religions still persist today.

FAITH

Religious faith embodies more than belief; consider it belief-plus. Faith elevates the follower by promising a particular outcome as a result of having that faith. It might be defined along the lines of having knowledge of the unknowable which is in turn 'verified' by having that faith, which is very much a circular definition.

Faith is not based on anything rational, but those who are able to put rationality aside and actually accept and internalize it achieve a great sense of wellbeing and comfort as a result. Christianity is unique amongst the traditional religions, differing even from those of the same Abrahamic root, in that its followers are defined by faith rather than belief. St Paul made this distinction when he wrote that belief (he used the words, "the law") was analogous to a tutor until Christ came along and replaced belief with faith, "when we should be justified through faith," and since Christ had replaced belief with faith the tutor was then no longer needed.

Christian faith is defined in The King James Version of the bible as: Faith is the substance of things hoped for, the evidence of things not seen. Etymologically, the word 'faith' is closely linked to fidelity, which emphasizes commitment to something or someone, in this case specifically to Christ. Thus, faith is often understood to mean 'loyalty' to that particular divinity.

The other two Abrahamic religions, Judaism and Islam, do not embody the concept of faith and require their followers to adhere to their belief systems, or obey the law. The word 'Islam' itself means 'submission to God'.

Faith gives Christians a spiritual component which provides them with more than the sense of belonging and comfort that comes from just belief. Faith gives them the 'knowledge' that there is a better life to come, a life after death. This is a concept that has made Christianity an extremely popular religion during the past two thousand years. St Paul identified faith, hope and charity as the three greatest virtues that are central to Christianity, and this idea is repeated and elaborated upon throughout Christian tradition. Faith is put first because it provides the foundation upon which the other two are built.

Christianity is not just defined by faith, however, but it also demands it; the importance of which was explained by Martin Luther in his Table Talk papers where he wrote:

"This is the acme of faith, to believe that God, who saves so few and condemns so many, is merciful; that he is just who, at his own pleasure, has made us necessarily doomed to damnation, so that he seems to delight in the torture of the wretched and is more deserving of hate than of love. If by any effort of reason, I could conceive how God, who shows so much anger and harshness, could be merciful and just, there would be no need of faith... "

Like belief, faith is a delusion. Karl Marx made the analogy that faith was like getting a prescription for an opiate from a doctor: an authority figure giving a person something that doesn't solve the problem but will make them feel good and help them to deal with their lives better.

RELIGIOUS BEHAVIOR

Belief and faith also direct followers as to how to interact with others. Depending upon their religion, people will either approach other individuals with either an exclusive or an inclusive orientation.

People with exclusive beliefs typically explain other religions as either being in error or as corruptions of the true faith. This approach is primarily seen with the fundamentalist and orthodox religions, and monotheist religions are often characterized by their rejection of other religions. All three Abrahamic monotheistic religions attest to the primacy of their religious writing and claim to have a monopoly on truth, with followers of the orthodox Christian religions often disparaging people from differing beliefs, considering them heretics and attempting to convert them.

People with inclusive beliefs are willing to recognize other religions and will attempt to focus on the things they have in common while minimizing any differences. Individuals who subscribe to blended religions and some of the more modern ones will typically be inclusive in their attitudes towards others. Followers of the Bahá'í religion consider that there is truth in all belief systems.

RELIGIOUS PRACTICE

Being a member of a particular religion and outwardly practicing it does not necessarily mean that the participant is actually a believer; the reality is that many of the practitioners of any particular religion today may just be going through the motions. The philosopher Margaret Gilbert explains this by suggesting that individuals who together collectively believe something need not personally believe it themselves.

Many of these established religions have been around for hundreds, in some cases thousands, of years, so why are they now experiencing a breakdown of belief with their individual participants? The answer lies in the nature of the modern world itself. While religious beliefs vary considerably, these differences were never much of an issue to the individual in the past when societies were homogeneous, and people rarely traveled far from home. However, in our interconnected modern world people are continually moving around and communicating with others via the internet. And, wherever they go, or whoever they talk to, they are taking their religious beliefs with them. This results in people being exposed to other belief systems, which in some cases has the potential to cause conflict for the individual when they realize that there are alternative ways to look at the world. Also, increased communication, especially with the widespread nature of social media, means that people are being exposed to new information and scientific discoveries on an almost daily basis. While increased knowledge and more information about the world is certainly a positive occurrence, in many cases it too is causing people to question what their particular religions may have led them to believe.

Religious organizations are undoubtedly aware of the growing feelings of angst within their membership, but their inflexible, static belief systems cause them to answer any and all questions with outdated rote. When people reach out to their religious leaders today in search of answers these traditional solutions are more likely to result in more angst, possibly even compounding it with a sense of guilt about the "incorrect thinking" which many individuals find they can do nothing about. Dissatisfied and not willing to simply stop thinking, these now disenchanted individuals realize that official doctrine does not agree with their privately developed 'beliefs' and they wrestle with what to do about it. With old religious doctrine no longer working for them as they try to make sense of the modern world, many people choose to stop believing in their religion, but they do continue to participate in it. Others, however, feel that doing so would be hypocritical, which explains the growing religious exodus that we are currently witnessing.

Why do non-believers continue to go through the motions of religious practice? The answer is probably some combination of there being a need for a sense of belonging, a social fit as mentioned previously, combined with the lack of a better alternative. It is easier to stay with something known, in spite of the fact it doesn't quite work, that to seek out something new.

There is another way that the individual can deal with all of this, however. Existential humanism doesn't require any belief system and instead focuses on the authentic individual freely pursuing truth through reason. Since it can be challenging to deal with people whose perspectives are based on belief or faith as opposed to rationality, existential humanists do not try to reconcile with them. Rather, we make no distinction between belief systems and simply recognize the importance of all of these differing religious beliefs in human societies. Every religion has inherent worth in that it provides its members with meaning, comfort, and purpose. Existential humanism is for those who are not interested in the comfort obtained from deluding themselves with belief systems or irrational faith. It works for people who desire a sense of wellbeing and a working understanding of the world they inhabit, while at the same time still questioning everything.

Chapter 7: Truth

The author, Salman Rushdie, wrote:

". . . I distrust people who claim to know the whole truth and who seek to orchestrate the world in line with that one true truth. I think that's a very dangerous position in the world. It needs to be challenged..."

WHAT IS TRUTH?

It may well be argued that one of the greatest drives the human species possesses is the seemingly innate desire to ask questions and search for truth in hope of trying to understand the nature of reality and how they as individuals fit into the universe. This searching can be broken down into three different categories: the truth about ourselves, the truth about the world we live in, and the truth about the universe, or infinity.

Let's first consider truth about ourselves. From the ancient Greek concept of fate to the myriad of theistic beliefs that a deity has a plan for each individual, the belief that human life is predetermined permeates many religions. Such belief is not truth, however, and understanding that life has no predetermined purpose and that as free individuals we are able to do with our lives what we wish can be a most liberating concept for many people. In the previous chapter about existentialism, we discussed the search for meaning and the importance of defining one's own life purpose, or as Socrates would have put it, to know ourselves. This is the truth about ourselves, our inner truth, and it is quite subjective because we create ourselves to be the unique individuals that we wish to be.

Once we understand this inner truth and proceed to live our lives in a manner that is consistent with it in order to be authentic, we will have eliminated many sources of stress in our lives.

It is important to recognize that subjectivity can only be applied to ourselves, however. When we are dealing with the world around us, we must deal with objective truth.

In the world around us, however, this objective truth is actually a transient axiom. Truth about the world around us can quite easily be defined as the best explanation we have for a situation, such that when we apply all of the knowledge available to us it cannot be logically refuted. Since new discoveries are adding to that pool of knowledge on a continual basis, we must accept that today's truth will only hold until a better explanation comes along, and yesterday's truth should already be considered suspect. All truths are therefore both objective and transient, and it is through having an open mind and questioning everything that individuals are free to not only better understand, but to also add to the collective knowledge of humanity. This brings us to the curious human dichotomy regarding the search for truth.

While we have the innate drive to ask questions in order to seek out what is true, we also hold steadfastly onto what he have already accepted and seem unwilling to let it go, even in the face of overwhelming evidence otherwise. This is actually a good trait amongst scientists because it ensures that new truths must be well established by repetitive experiment and observation, a process known as scientific proof, before they gain acceptance. A newly discovered truth is not something that is readily accepted and it must win the argument before rational minds permit it to displace the old thinking. This process ensures that we don't randomly flit from one 'truth' to another and only advance to the next truth when it has been sufficiently proven.

EXISTENTIAL HUMANISM: HOW TO LIVE AUTHENTICALLY IN TODAY'S WORLD

Certainly, if you examine the fields of mathematics and physics you'll recognize some truths that have been with us for centuries, but how many more have been replaced in that time? The earth is neither flat nor is it the center of the universe (although if you choose to believe such things that is entirely your choice).

Recognizing that truth necessarily goes through an arduous process before being accepted by even the most rational minds, who have to override their internal resistance to something new, one can begin to understand why many of the old 'truths' not only still remain but are widely accepted in our societies. Within those societies the individual search for truth has been discouraged for millennia by religions who train its members from early childhood to repress that innate drive in favor of following the collective creed. Rather than embrace emerging knowledge, most of the religious institutions that people turn to for answers view new ideas and truths as threats and they use the naturally occurring human resistance to change in their followers to their advantage. Preying on the uncertainty of the unknown, these religions repeatedly bombard their followers with the same stories and songs which have been a source of comfort for many of them since childhood, sometimes reinforcing them by the threat of what may happen to those who do not believe. In this way they have been generally successful at keeping their membership. So, while many human beings will outwardly attest to being open minded and are supposedly searching for truth, they are, in fact, clinging to anachronisms and are really afraid to even consider alternatives lest they see something that may challenge what they choose, or have been trained, to believe to be true. While established religions do provide serenity and comfort, is it really in the best interests of people today to cling to these ideologies? Embracing them simply because they are traditional and sacred and allowing them to subvert their rationality?

For many years religious groups have been successful at suppressing and withholding new information from even reaching the majority of its membership, but that is not the case in today's world. With such free and available access to information that we now enjoy it follows that more and more humans are beginning to question the so called truths they have been raised with, even recognizing that there is no such thing as an all-encompassing, universal truth. One might well argue that for many the reason for doing so is driven by culture, from a desire to be an accepted member of a particular group. But if a person can no longer believe they will experience inner conflict; the angst mentioned previously that drives people to leave their established religion.

The truth about the world around us is therefore objective, and the scientific method is a tool that provides us with the means to discovering it. In the world around us, truth must be realized objectively while recognizing that today's truth may only be transient.

But what about infinity? As ancient humans observed the world, they noticed an apparent sense of order in that things begin and end, live and die, and so people naturally began to wonder about the causes of these naturally occurring events. Being able to understand the changes of seasons, when it would rain and when rivers would flood would have immense importance to early agricultural communities. Extrapolating from cause and effect that humans observed in their daily lives they concluded that these events must be due to the actions other beings, which they called gods, which at the time would have provided a satisfying explanation. Supernatural explanations have served to fill the void of not knowing ever since; they could be looked at as placeholders until a better explanation comes up.

Fast forward to today and one can see that advances in science have displaced much of the old need for gods. Humans currently have a pretty good handle on truth about the way things work in our world. But those same truths do not necessarily apply to the rest of the universe.

It is important to recognize that we are finite beings living on a finite planet in our finite, measurable, universe. But the universe as a whole is infinite and infinity is something that is conceptually difficult for people to understand. Consider, we know that life appeared on earth about 3.7 billion years ago, the earth is about 4.5 billion years old, and our universe came into existence about 13.8 billion years ago. The question of origin, creation, asks about what existed before our universe came into being and what is outside our known universe. This thinking leads us to try to figure out the origin of everything; perhaps the hardest question that humanity currently wrestles with. But by definition there is no origin to infinity, so this type of question doesn't apply to anything outside our own universe.

The big bang theory provides a useful conceptual framework to describe the origins of our particular universe and helps to predict what may happen to it in the future, but in order to develop a working understanding of infinity it is important to think of the big bang simply as a transition of part of it into something finite: measurable space and time.

Humans require a conceptual framework, things like space, time, energy fields, for reason to be able to function, but these things are irrelevant to infinity. But even though the origin/creation question is a product of very human thought processes and therefore applicable only to things within our finite universe, we are still able to satisfy it in one of two ways. One can either avoid thinking by ascribing the answer to an unknowable god, as many people do, or one can develop a working understanding of infinity. A person does not need to be an astrophysicist for the latter, just examine what it is that they do know.

Consider the following working model which enables this author to reconcile infinity for himself which can be summarized as: the truth of infinity is that all is nothing is everything.

We know about matter and antimatter, and that when identical particles of matter and antimatter are brought together, they annihilate each other, and nothing remains. Far from being a science-fiction concept, we not only know that antimatter exists, but it is being used every day in modern medicine. PET, positron emission tomography, uses positrons, which are anti-electrons, to produce high-resolution images of the body. Positron-emitting radioactive isotopes are attached to chemicals such as glucose that are used naturally by the body. These are then injected into the bloodstream where they are naturally broken down, and when these positrons meet electrons in the body they annihilate each other. These annihilations produce gamma rays that are used to construct images. Scientists are also studying antimatter as a potential way to treat cancer.

While we and our world/universe are made up of matter, we can also infer the existence of other finite universes that are made up of antimatter. If an identical matter and an antimatter universe were to collide there would be nothing left, but if they are not absolutely identical then the resultant destruction could be something akin to another big bang. Depending on whether there was more matter or antimatter in that collision, then the result might be a new, finite, matter or an antimatter universe. This is not inconsistent with current theory which acknowledges that the only reason our universe exists was that the big bang released more matter than antimatter.

Considering that infinity contains an infinite amount of matter and antimatter in equal quantities, that time only occurs in finite universes and does not exist in infinity, then infinity may exist simultaneously as both everything and nothing. Since this author considers this a logically derived theory based on what we know, or can infer from what we know, he therefore considers it to be true. This answer to the question of creation, as presented above as the truth of infinity, is not something we are (yet) able to apply the scientific method to, but the fact it is derived rationally may prove to be a satisfactory answer for those who do not wish to fall back on superstition.

Chapter 8: Science

"The good thing about science is that it's true whether or not you believe in it." — Neil deGrasse Tyson

SCIENCE AND RELIGION

In spite of the way it is so often positioned in the media, science is neither the opposite of nor is it opposed to religion. Science is simply the tool that humans use to search for truth. In fact, science has historically been sponsored by religions that have used it as a means to study the laws behind creation.

While there have been significant clashes throughout history between Christianity and the emergence of new truths that science uncovers before they gain acceptance, the current so-called religion versus science debate is really not reflective of Christian religions as a whole. Much of this is the result of clashes between zealous Christian fundamentalists and militant atheists which are well publicized in the media and used by politicians for personal gain. Mainstream Christianity has pretty much accepted that evolution can fit in with their views of the universe, for instance, but a number of people representing the religious right, mainly in the United States, vehemently oppose evolution and threatens eternal damnation to anyone' who does not accept their version of creation. In reality the religion versus science debate is simply propaganda supporting a hidden agenda with the main fuel behind it being politicians seeking easy votes. This has allowed the promotion of the views of both Christian fundamentalists and militant atheists via their publicity machines. Both sides take positions of support behind these two extremes to manipulate the media.

51

HISTORY OF SCIENCE AND CHRISTIANITY

The beginnings of science may be attributed to Aristotle, who proposed that truth was to be learned through the things we can see, hear, feel, taste, and smell. His method of learning stated that rather than looking to some heavenly principle to determine the meaning of things on earth, as promoted by Plato, we should observe the things around us in order to be able understand them. According to Aristotle, truth was to be found through the senses rather than being revealed by a god. However, since his writings were 'lost' (more likely, suppressed) during the early history of the church, his thinking did not have as much impact as Plato's in the development of Christianity.

Christianity became well established throughout Europe during the dark ages, and by the middle ages Christian dogma stated that the bible should be read literally and that any alternative viewpoint was heresy. Despite this, after Aristotle's works were re-discovered there were large numbers of people throughout Europe developing theories and pursuing science, many of whom were monks not only supported but also encouraged by the Christian church. It wasn't until the 14 th-15th centuries before the truths uncovered by science began to challenge official church doctrine.

The first well documented challenge came from Nicolaus Copernicus, who postulated the idea that the earth revolved around the sun. This was considered to be a direct affront to Christianity, which at the time believed that the earth was the center of the universe. By the time Giordano Bruno came along and expanded upon Copernicus' ideas that other stars may have worlds revolving around them, scientific challenges had the church leaders seriously worried that their dogma was going to be undermined. In response, they made death the punishment for heresy, and proceeded to burn Bruno at the stake. The Inquisition was then established to enforce Christian doctrine, officially authorized to torture or kill anyone who dared to challenge it.

However, even the threat of the Inquisition failed to stop some people from questioning and pursuing scientific thought, as demonstrated by Galileo, perhaps the most famous scientist of his time and someone the Inquisition sought to make an example of. In 1611 Galileo first came to the attention of the Inquisition for his Copernican views. They developed their case against him and in 1616 Galileo was called to the residence of Pope Paul V where he was told that the proposition that the sun was the center of the universe and that the earth has an annual motion around it was absurd, and that the Inquisition considered it to be heresy. The pope assured Galileo that he had not been on trial, nor was being condemned by the Inquisition, provided that he no longer discussed the theory orally or in writing. It was prudent of Galileo to go along with this at the time, waiting until 1624 before he was again able to publish his work after he successfully appealed to Pope Urban VIII by promising to treat the Copernican theory as simply a mathematical hypothesis.

Galileo ran afoul of the Inquisition again in 1625 with his publication of *The Assayer,* in which he supported the atomistic theory. This was a theory originally proposed by Democritus, an ancient Greek, who stated that matter was composed of small particles which he called atoms. The Inquisition argued that atomism cannot be reconciled with the official church doctrine regarding the Eucharist, in which bread and wine are ``transubstantiated" into Christ's flesh and blood. Galileo, probably by leveraging on his friendship with Pope Urban VIII, was eventually cleared after an investigation.

Then, in 1630, he completed a book in which he discussed and compared the Copernican model and the church approved Ptolemaic model, which caused him to be summoned to Rome to once again face the

Inquisition in 1633. Under formal interrogation and threat of torture he confessed that he may have made the Copernican case too strong. He was subsequently placed under house arrest in Sienna, where he remained until his death in 1642, and this book was never published.

There is an argument to be made that when the Reformation occurred, it was an attempt to throw off some of the restrictions of Catholicism and push back against the Inquisition. The resulting emergence of Protestantism once again enabled Christianity to become more open to science. Christian scientist-philosophers, such as René Descartes in the 17th century, then became quite successful in showing that the study of the law behind divine creation was not heretical.

The work of Isaac Newton may be considered the first publicized challenge to the church, and his formulas demonstrating a predictable understanding of the world around us became a landmark for physics going forward. People became increasingly confident in human ability to explain the world apart from divine revelation, and they also began to become increasingly optimistic about their ability to improve the world.

This led some Christian churches to concede that the world can be explained sufficiently through science, while at the same time maintaining that the Christian religion was still important for a spiritual life. Essentially, the church adapted by deciding that there were two types of things in the world, spiritual things and natural things, and there were two separate ways of knowing those two types of things, belief/faith and science. If you refer back to the chapter on truth, these natural things are synonymous with the real world and the spiritual things the church was referring to are the truths about the individual, the meaning of life, and creation, or universe and infinity.

Many scientists have been quite successful in reconciling their Christian beliefs with science and have proceeded to make tremendous contributions to humanity. Gregor Mendel was an Austrian monk who first proposed the basis of heredity and spawned the science of genetics, and the first advocate of the Big Bang theory was a Roman Catholic priest named Georges Lemaître who wrote about a 'creation event' at the beginning of the universe.

So where does the current science versus religion, specifically Christianity, debate come from? Most Christians today accept that their faith is personal and does not belong in politics, but a fundamentalist faction called the creationists have tried to reconcile their ideas into a pseudo-scientific format which they call Intelligent Design. Intelligent Designs holds the view that the biblical story of creation is the literal truth. They have brought their argument into the political forefront, and militant atheists have responded in kind, which has resulted in the media sensationalism. Even though Charles Darwin was a Christian, it is his theories of evolution and natural selection that have become the fuel for this needless debate between creationists and evolutionists.

SCIENTIFIC PROGRESS

Scientific progress doesn't happen as smoothly as one might imagine because it requires objectivity. Scientists are also human beings, to whom objectivity doesn't come easily. Personal desires and cultural influences can easily influence their interpretations of natural phenomena, and combined with the fact that humans also have a tendency to cling to old truths it can often take many years for a new truth to displace them. In order to minimize this human factor, science strives for clarity by using a system of scientific concepts and language to obtain the truth from particular observations.

Unlike our everyday languages, scientific language is international and is in constant development by people from all parts of the world. The scientist develops theories and works in solitude, but it is through the common language of science that new ideas can be shared with the rest of the world. It is then from the subsequent cooperative efforts of others who test, confirm and tweak, that we are able to discover the truths which have transformed the lives of human beings over the past centuries. It is important, however, to recognize that science is only a tool which provides the mechanism for discovery. Science by itself has no ability to produce anything without the human input of questioning.

Over the centuries the scientific method has become well honed, but how effectively it is used is completely dependent upon the questions that humans ask. Simply following the scientific method does not always ensure that human bias is completely removed either. There will always be opposition to a new truth before it can displace an existing one as scientists seek to use those same tools to make adjustments to their old theories in order to preserve them. Taking a look at the old phlogiston theory and the current dark matter theory provides wonderful examples of how science is a constant work in motion.

THE PHLOGISTON THEORY

The phlogiston theory, first proposed by Johann Becher in 1667, was a scientific attempt to explain the process of burning. Becher theorized that that there was an element contained within combustible materials that was released during combustion, and in 1703 Georg Stahl named this substance phlogiston. Phlogisticated substances were substances that contained phlogiston and they dephlogisticated when burned by releasing the phlogiston inside, which was absorbed by the air. Growing plants then absorbed this phlogiston, which is why air does not spontaneously combust and also why plant matter burns as well as it does. Wood was, therefore, just a combination of ash and plogiston.

EXISTENTIAL HUMANISM: HOW TO LIVE AUTHENTICALLY IN TODAY'S WORLD

In general, substances that burned in air were said to be rich in phlogiston, and the fact that combustion soon ceased in an enclosed space was taken as clear-cut evidence that air had the capacity to absorb only a finite amount of phlogiston. When air had become completely phlogisticated it would no longer serve to support combustion of any material, nor could phlogisticated air support life. Breathing was thought to take phlogiston out of the body.

J. H. Pott, expanded on this theory and attempted to make it much more understandable to people. He compared phlogiston to light, it being a substance that everyone knows what it is but cannot give an entirely satisfactory definition. He thought that phlogiston should not be considered to be a particle but an essence that permeates substances.

Scientific experimentation eventually revealed problems with this version of the phlogiston theory, including the fact that some metals gained mass when they burned, and burning was not always accompanied by a loss of material. In order to reconcile the theory with observation, Johann Juncker concluded that phlogiston has the property of levity, or that it makes the compound that it is in much lighter than it would be without the phlogiston.

Other phlogiston proponents explained this by concluding that phlogiston had negative mass, while Louis-Bernard Guyton de Morveau gave the more conventional argument that phlogiston was lighter than air.

During the 18th century phlogiston was increasingly regarded as a principle rather than a material substance, and by the end of the century the few chemists who still used the term phlogiston had linked it to hydrogen. Joseph Priestley, for example, in referring to the reaction of steam on iron to form iron oxide, said that iron also loses "the basis of inflammable air (hydrogen), and this is the substance or principle, to which we give the name phlogiston."

Phlogiston remained the dominant theory until the 1780s when Antoine-Laurent Lavoisier, widely considered to be the originator of modern chemistry, showed that combustion requires a gas that has mass which he called oxygen.

The scientists who supported the phlogiston theory attempted to respond to Lavoisier's competing oxygen theory by revising their theories on phlogiston in order to make them work with what Lavoisier was doing in his experiments, but ended up making the phlogiston theory so complex that it eventually fell out of favor and faded away. The burning processes, such as combustion and rusting, then became known as oxidation.

For over a hundred years the phlogiston theory was true because it was the best explanation available based on what was known, and this brief history of it shows the reluctance of scientists to give up on it when the oxidation theory attempted to displace it. A similar scenario may be happening today as scientists try to explain why over 80% of the matter that is supposed to be in our universe appears to be missing.

DARK MATTER

The current cosmological model of our universe is that it began with a big bang, but astrophysicists have been unable to reconcile the universe they can observe with its movement. According to their calculations, almost 85% of the mass of the universe must be invisible, and they have called this invisible material dark matter. No one has ever detected dark matter, but scientists infer its presence by the fact it exerts a huge gravitational pull which moves and shapes our galaxy and the galaxies around us. Without the presence of dark matter there is no way the observed matter contained in galaxies would generate enough gravity to keep the stars locked in their orbits.

A problem with this dark matter, however, is that doesn't seem to interact with stars, planets, dust, atoms, subatomic particles, or any other matter that we know about. All it has is gravity, and a lot of it. Astrophysics' current theory is that dark matter could be comprised of what they call weakly interacting massive particles, or WIMPS, and to test this theory they built an incredibly sensitive Large Underground Xenon, LUX, dark-matter detector, buried under a mile of rock, to search for them.

Scientists "pushed the sensitivity of the instrument to a final performance level that is four times better than the original project goals" over a period of 20 months which ended in 2016. They found nothing, which perhaps indicates that it may be about time to switch to a new theory that is not based on something that isn't there. There is an alternative theory which has been proposed by cosmologist Alexander Kashlinsky who suggests that the gravity acting on our universe may not be due to particles at all, but to gravitational waves. The recent discovery of gravitational waves brought about by the collision of two massive black holes supports the theory that dark matter is not real, and that the majority of the matter in our universe simply exists within black holes, which renders it unobservable. Most of the gravity which is acting on the galaxies around us, therefore, could be coming from countless such black holes.

But after over 30 years of dark matter being the prevailing theory many scientists are holding out hope that upgraded versions of the experiments looking for WIMPs will find them. A lot of time, money, and effort has already been spent looking for it. Cosmologists need dark matter to make their interpretations of the big bang work, and subsequently to keep their biases and reputations intact. As a result, a next-generation LUX detector is currently being built which may be able to achieve 70 times the sensitivity of the current LUX. Sooner or later, though, scientists may have to accept the possibility that dark matter does not exist and concentrate their search for truth elsewhere. Perhaps gravitational waves or something new which has yet to be proposed.

OBJECTIVITY

The historical example of phlogiston has shown that wrong paradigms can prevail for decades or centuries, and the current dark matter theory may very likely turn out to be the modern equivalent of phlogiston. Science is a tool to search for truth, but for it to be used successfully it is important not to let human bias interfere with objectivity.

Chapter 9: Other People

THE WORLD IS FULL OF OTHER PEOPLE

As we experience the world around us we recognize everything in it as objects which we can use as tools to achieve our goals, and from this perspective the world really is our own. We also view other people in the same fashion, objectifying them and placing them as we wish in our world when we view them from a distance. For instance, when we see a dentist or a plumber or an auto mechanic we think of them in utilitarian terms as someone who can check our teeth, fix the faucet in our tub, or change the oil in our car, and we categorize them as to our perceptions of what a dentist, plumber or auto mechanic should be.

But when we interact with another person we become aware that they are seeing us in the same manner as we see them, and we recognize that we are as much an object in that person's world as they are in ours. This means that they have formed an opinion of us based on what they have observed, and we may furthermore realize that this other person's opinion might actually matter to us. Yet if we allow another person's judgment of us to be important, it follows that they can influence us and cause us to alter our behavior, possibly moving us towards acting inauthentically.

Jean-Paul Sartre created a now famous illustration to demonstrate how a person's world can collapse under the influence of another:

"Let us imagine that moved by jealousy, curiosity, or vice I have just glued my ear to the door and looked through a keyhole." While this individual is alone he is free to objectify whoever is present in that room with no effect on his perception of himself, "a pure consciousness of things." However, as soon as he hears footsteps in the hall and realizes that he has been seen, the situation changes radically; by being looked at he has become solidified into the role of a peeping Tom. "Beyond any knowledge which I can have, I am this self whom another knows. And this self which I am – this I am in a world which the Other has made alien to me, for the Other's look embraces my being and correlatively the walls, the door, the keyhole."

Allowing another person's judgment to be important to us is what Sartre was referring to in his play, *No Exit*, with his well-known quote, 'Hell is other people." It is only in solitude that an individual can be closest to their authentic self, but unless we isolate ourselves we must necessarily encounter, and therefore interact with, other people in the world around us.

LIVING AUTHENTICALLY AROUND OTHERS

Other people see us in a ways that we have no access to, and vice-versa. We are first and foremost an object to other people, just as they are to us, and according to Jean-Paul Sartre this is the basis for relationships between individuals to be one of conflict. Other people cannot see us as we really are, so our existence is one thing for us and something else for them. If we allow the judgment of others to influence us we run the risk of not being authentic and will experience stress as a result. So how can one be a part of the world and live authentically at the same time?

We can try to tell people who we really are, but it is only through our actions and the products of our actions that they will judge us. Consider a man who is living in a shack on the beach. Other people see this person with a scraggly beard and long hair blowing in the breeze walking around every day and they label him as a beach bum. They are unaware that it is the daily wandering that drives his inspiration and creativity, and even if he told them that he was a genius working on a new project they would most likely look at him askance and still judge him to be a beach bum. However, once he publishes a book or produces a painting these people will change their judgment, and from that point on they'll recognize him as an author or an artist.

It is one thing to see ourselves as artists and tell other people at parties how we have great books or paintings inside us, but quite another to actually be that artist. That requires us to make choices and act on them. So whether we remain as inwardly frustrated artists who dress in suits and go to work in an office every day versus living an authentic life and producing art comes down to our accepting individual freedom and making the appropriate choices, in spite of the judgment of others.

It is easy to come up with excuses in order to justify not taking action, but Nietzsche would have considered it weakness to deny ourselves when he wrote:

"What is good? All that heightens the feeling of power, the will to power, power itself. What is bad? All that is born of weakness. What is happiness? The feeling that power is growing, that resistance is overcome."

You may well be considered a nonconformist bum when you start out, but those same people who deride your choices will be the first ones with their congratulations on your success. And will readily accept what they will then consider your eccentricity. More importantly, you will achieve happiness and be free of the stress of inauthenticity.

RELATIONSHIPS WITHOUT FRUSTRATION

While recognizing that relationships with other people are going to essentially produce conflict and frustration, we must also consider how they are nevertheless important to us. Certainly the strongest relationships come about where each participant wholeheartedly throws themselves into the relationship, but while doing it is still important to retain one's own sense of self. By allowing each other the freedom to pursue their own goals and interests, relationships can be of tremendous benefit to both parties and can actually add more meaning to our lives. Unfortunately, people too often use relationships with others as an escape from the world. According to Simone de Beauvoir, the feeling of security may be comforting, but it becomes problematic when people make the relationship the only source of meaning in their lives. Instead, she advised people not to become so dependent on one another that they can't exist without each other.

Relationships are more interesting and stronger if the participants pursue rich and diversified lives through their own authentic projects. In this way they are free to focus their energies on concurrent flourishing and supporting each other's goals, instead of holding each other down with petty power games. Relationships can have so much more to them if the participants are strong-willed and are good friends.

Unfortunately, there is a common theme in western culture around the idea of finding what is referred to as a soulmate; that somehow there are people in the world who were "made for each other" and destined to be together. Since individuals are free and must therefore define themselves (existence precedes essence), there can obviously be no such things as soulmates. Not only is this a useless romantic illusion, it is also dangerous.

De Beauvoir argued that a belief in soulmateship seduces lovers into turning away from their own authentic goals for the sake of the relationship. Lovers are first and foremost individuals who should take responsibility for creating their own lives and not become reliant on a relationship with another person to be their meaning in life. The best kinds of lovers, therefore, respect each other's freedom and support each other's flourishing and striving towards whatever goals the individuals choose, even if it means pursuing goals that may ultimately pull them in different directions.

Being an authentic individual in no way detracts from the pleasures of being involved in a loving relationship, and there can be no better example of this than the love story of Jean-Paul Sartre and Simone de Beauvoir. We know much about their relationship from de Beauvoir's memoirs and the letters they wrote to each other, which were published after their deaths.

They met as young philosophy students and remained lifelong companions while living and loving with complete transparency. Shunning marriage and monogamy, they refused the hypocrisy of convention while enjoying the stability and commitment to each other that comes with a solid relationship. In modern terminology we would consider them to be the epitome of sapiosexuals: intellectual equals who respected and encouraged each other in every way. Recognizing that authentic love would not try to rob the other of their freedom, they even gave each other the freedom to fall in love with other people and then shared every emotion and sensation with each other in marathon, analytical conversations. On several occasions, de Beauvoir began an affair with one of her female students and then passed her lover along to Sartre, providing fodder for them to intellectually dissect.

Jean-Paul Sartre was by no means a handsome man, but he was intellectually brilliant and a captivating talker who routinely seduced women with his words. He had an insatiable need for other women and enjoyed many mistresses, but sex with them was secondary to the subsequent analysis he shared with de Beauvoir over drinks at a Paris cafe.

De Beauvoir and Sartre enjoyed a mutually satisfying existential loving relationship for most of their lives. Hell may be other people, but their relationship was probably the closest thing to heaven for the two of them.

Jean-Paul Sartre and Simone de Beauvoir were existentialists, not humanists, and they left a lot of human wreckage in the wake of their relationship as demonstrated by what happened to two of the women they were involved with. Bianca Lamblin, one of de Beauvoir's young lovers whom she shared with Sartre, experienced a nervous breakdown after being involved with the two of them. And Evelyne Rey, one of Sartre's love-struck mistresses, committed suicide.

Sartre may have grappled with humanistic aspects which may be why he supported several of his mistresses financially, but de Beauvoir simply shrugged this off as his attempt to appease a guilty conscience.

While a Sartre-de Beauvoir like relationship is undoubtedly appealing, adding a humanist component could still enable one to enjoy a frustration free relationship without the potential of harming others. While we cannot know for sure, but perhaps if they had more compassion towards the other women in their lives they might have avoided some of the consequences.

Perfect relationships with others, therefore, includes the existential ideal of remaining an authentic person while recognizing and supporting one's partner's goals, friendship and open communication, and also a humanistic consideration for others.

Unlike Sartre and de Beauvoir, many authentic individuals do include marriage and monogamy in their relationships. The important consideration is that they do so because it is a good fit for their particular relationship, rather than doing so because of societal pressure. If entered into for external reasons, marriage may be become viewed as ownership which deteriorates into obligation and monogamy may soon lead to infidelity; both most definitely sources of frustration.

COMMUNITY

One of the appealing factors of religion is that it provides a sense of community, but there are so many alternative ways to be a part of a community in the modern world.

Communities in the past were defined geographically, but access to the internet has completely removed physical barriers to communication with other people and social media platforms currently comprise the largest communities in the world. Interest groups within these platforms enable people of like minds to correspond on a variety of topics that are relevant to them, no matter where they are in the world.

Similarly, direct interaction with other human beings no longer requires physically congregating in buildings or other physical locations. The internet provides us with the ability to speak to virtually anyone in the world in real time, and using free communications programs such as Skype we can even see who we are talking to and video conference several people together at the same time.

Not having the need for a physical structure as a place to meet has tremendously expanded our ability to engage directly with others.

The next best thing to actually conversing with someone is the ability to access their thoughts or point of view on a subject through their writings, and in this way the internet even enables us to 'communicate' with all of the humanity that has come before us. From this perspective, the library of the world that is the internet is an incredible time machine. Just type in to Google or your favorite search engine what is on your mind, such as Aristotle's take on spirit or Plato on reality, and you are immediately connected with their words. Search engines are sufficiently sophisticated that you can type in an inquiry with the same words that you would use if a person were right in front of you.

Using the search approach also provides another means to find your particular community. Whenever you perform a search on a particular topic you will also see other people's thoughts and interpretations by means of numerous posted articles, blogs and you-tube videos. You are free to both learn from these people as well as joining them in the conversation.

Since community is no longer defined by geographical location and communication with others does not require people to enter a physical structure, we can participate with others from the comfort of our own chairs and without having to dress for the occasion. Alone...yet connected.

Chapter 10: Who You Are

Who you are as an individual is so often not top of mind in day to day life. You need to be in the world to earn money to cover life's expenses, and the occupation you perform defines you to the world around you. You have been objectified, but chances are very good that you have also allowed that objectification to influence how you view yourself. So much so that you may have even come to internalize who you are with your occupation. But what you do is simply a means to an end, it is not who you are.

Acceptance of being objectified starts early in life with virtually every parent quite innocently asking their children the question, "What do you want to be when you grow up?" The answers generally come back as an occupation such as a doctor or an astronaut, but that isn't really the correct answer. The correct answer to that question should be, "Me." The parent asked the wrong question. What they should be asking is, "What do you want to DO when you grow up?"

Who you are is your authentic self, defined by you, but hidden from others in the world. You may not be consciously aware of it, but the products of your occupation are very likely tied to who you are. After necessary expenses you tend to spend your disposable income on what satisfies you and makes you happy. Since you derive benefits from the way you spend the money you earn, examining what those benefits are may help you to connect with your authentic self. Once you break who you are away from what you do, you can set goals that will provide you with true satisfaction in your life.

While you are free to make your own choices, it is obvious that the choices you do make will be influenced by the society and culture you are in, and that is fine. The key is to make the life that you want, and many of the things that influenced you prior to this point are important to you, so of course you're going to keep them. The key is to be able to first describe what the ideal life means to you and then determine how to live it. This isn't going to be physical things such as possessions, but how you want to feel. Knowing that, you can then examine the various ways to achieve those feelings. It is your responsibility to then get there, to do what it takes, to achieve it. This might at first seem risky, but isn't it a bigger risk is to plod along and end your life with the words "I wish I had" on your lips.

Also, it isn't the achievement of the goal that makes you free. It is the journey, knowing you are in control of your life, which makes it so. Remember the words of Frederick Nietzsche:

"Man is a rope stretched between the animal and the Superman — a rope over an abyss. A dangerous crossing, a dangerous wayfaring, a dangerous looking-back, a dangerous trembling and halting. What is great in man is that he is a bridge and not a goal."

GOALS

Goals should not be considered in light of external things but in the benefit those things give you. For instance, you may want to be, or even are, a lawyer. The benefit of being a lawyer might be the intellectual challenge it provides or the satisfaction gained from helping others. Yes, there is the income to consider, but money itself is never a goal, it is simply the intermediary means of exchange between what you do and what you desire. If you really think money should be a goal for you then I encourage you to look into the story of King Midas. Instead, drill down to find out what motivates you and what you really want in your life. Think about lifestyle and how you would like to feel every day. What does the money you are earning do for you now? Perhaps it enables you to take a vacation, two weeks of bliss on the beach. If while there you find you are truly happy and begin to dream of spending every day on the beach, for example, you may have discovered a true goal for your authentic self.

Set goals for what you want, but if you really want to achieve them then you must recognize that it will take action on your part. Consider these actions as paying your dues. Lots of people say they have goals, but without any action to back them up then those goals are just unachievable daydreams.

ACTION PLAN

Let's use the above benefit of being happy by spending every day on the beach as your goal, for example. You can then identify what you have to do in order to get there. This is called your action plan, and it is simply a series of sequential steps you'll need to follow.

You first calculate how much money you would need to live on if you spent every day on the beach. Next, you determine how you are going to earn it. Maybe being a lawyer is good because it can bring in a lot of money, so being a lawyer becomes an action that will help you to achieve your goal. The key here is that being a lawyer is no longer the goal, but part of the process to take you to your goal.

By staying focused on your goal you forgo frivolous purchases and willingly set aside the majority of the disposable income you make towards reaching it. So you play the role of a lawyer, and the world objectifies you as a lawyer, but you remain authentic by recognizing that this is what you need to be doing in order to be able to spend your life on the beach. What you do is not who you are. You can enjoy the process as you work towards your goals, and smile when you are objectified by others, because you know better.

In order to achieve a goal, an individual must rely on self-motivation. Remember that words and intentions are meaningless, it is only actions and results that matter. Action also cures fear. Look at the word FEAR as an acronym for "false evidence appearing real."

Refuse to cripple yourself by giving into fears and doubts and allowing excuses to prevent you from living the life you really want. Rely on your action plan as your guiding document. The American founding father, Thomas Jefferson, put it correctly when he penned: "life, liberty and the pursuit of happiness." in the declaration of independence. He knew it was all about the pursuit rather than an end product. If you do achieve one goal, you will undoubtedly come up with another.

Actually, Jefferson took this concept from John Locke, who wrote:

"The necessity of pursuing happiness [is] the foundation of liberty. As therefore the highest perfection of intellectual nature lies in a careful and constant pursuit of true and solid happiness; so the care of ourselves, that we mistake not imaginary for real happiness, is the necessary foundation of our liberty. The stronger ties we have to an unalterable pursuit of happiness in general, which is our greatest good, and which, as such, our desires always follow, the more are we free from any necessary determination of our will to any particular action..."

An existential humanist recognizes that freedom means life is unrestricted and he/she can do whatever they wish with it, and also accepts the personal responsibility to make it happen. Wishing for something to happen isn't going to do anything, and no external force is simply going to hand it to you. Your life is completely up to you, and you are solely responsible for it.

EXISTENTIAL HUMANISM: HOW TO LIVE AUTHENTICALLY IN TODAY'S WORLD

LIVING AN AUTHENTIC LIFE

How many people reading this would like to experience the feelings of freedom and wonder that they had as a child? Imagine those feelings without the need for a parental figure for support (you provide that for yourself) and without a parent controlling you. What does that tell you about who you really are? You may have wanted to grow up because you wanted to be free to make your own decisions, but did you in fact simply trade parents for bosses and other authority figures in your life?

Let me illustrate how this all works by using my story as an example:

Several years ago, in spite of the fact I had become a regional vice president of a national insurance company and was earning a good income, I hated where I was in life and dreamed of simply running away. My solution was to set a goal and follow the plan outlined above.

The goal I set was to regain childhood on my terms. I wanted a life of daily wonder and exploration, constant learning and intellectual stimulation, and to spend whole days enjoying nature, in a forest or on a beach, while disconnected from the rest of the world. I wanted independence with no external influences, and the freedom to enjoy solitude whenever I wished.

This life, of course, was going to require a decent chunk of money.

Since I naturally rebel against authority, which was one of the issues I had with my corporate position, and I had already realized that working for others would too stressful, I decided my best step would be to become some sort of an entrepreneur and go into business for myself. My role with the insurance company had introduced me to the life of an insurance broker, a person who had complete freedom of his time with unlimited income potential. Since I was familiar with the products, I quit my job and started my own brokerage.

The first few years were grueling and I needed daily escape, which I had always done by reading, and I also began to write, something I was always good at in school and dreamed of doing when I was older. Poetry and short stories provided me with the perfect escape mechanism because I was able to enter into the world of my imagination and leave the real world behind me while I did so. It occurred to me that being an author would also fit nicely into my perfect life when I arrived there, so this became another goal. If I published, there would also be an income stream from it; this plan was getting better all the time. I wouldn't be dependent upon the money I socked away as an insurance broker.

To cut a long story short, after living frugally and keeping my eye-on-the-ball, I was able to sell my insurance brokerage and move to the Bahamas to live. I was on the beach in a short 10 minute walk, and I had a writing studio where I could disappear undisturbed into the worlds of my imagination at any time.

Keep in mind that this goal had to be secret until it was achieved. While I was following my action pan, the world saw me, objectified me, as a successful businessman. Nobody would have guessed that the real me was a kid playing on the beach and enjoying an imaginary world. I visited this world every day in my head, which helped me to keep going on my action plan.

I lived in the Bahamas for 3 delightful years before developing another goal, which has now relocated me in the United States of America.

I thoroughly enjoy my life, and I have a fully working understanding of what life is. I am a perpetual student, constantly seeking out new information and updating my world view when I come across knowledge that expands it.

EXISTENTIAL HUMANISM: HOW TO LIVE AUTHENTICALLY IN TODAY'S WORLD

I am also a teacher, sharing what I have learned with interested others, and in this way may be able to contribute to the progression of humanity.

I have no need for superstition or rote belief in anything. I live my life on my own terms.

I am an advocate of individual freedom and its necessary companion, personal responsibility.

I will end with a quote from Carl Sagan:

"The significance of our lives and our fragile planet is then determined only by our own wisdom and courage. We are the custodians of life's meaning. We long for a parent to care for us, to forgive us our errors, to save us from our childish mistakes. But knowledge is preferable to ignorance. Better by far to embrace the hard truth than a reassuring fable. If we crave some cosmic purpose, then let us find ourselves a worthy goal."

About the Author

Ronald thoroughly enjoys his life and has a fully working understanding of what life is. He is a perpetual student, constantly seeking out new information and updating his world view when he comes across knowledge that expands it.

He is also a teacher, sharing what he has learned with interested others, and in this way may be able to contribute to the progression of humanity.

He has no need for superstition or rote belief in anything, and lives life on his own terms.

He is a firm advocate of individual freedom and its necessary companion, personal responsibility.

Read more at https://ronaldhaines.com.

.

www.ingramcontent.com/pod-product-compliance
Lightning Source LLC
Chambersburg PA
CBHW060555100426
42742CB00013B/2565